DATES IN THE STATES

A COUPLE TRAVELING THE UNITED
STATES ON A BUDGET

I0541636

Mystery Date
Victor, NY

By Dates in the States

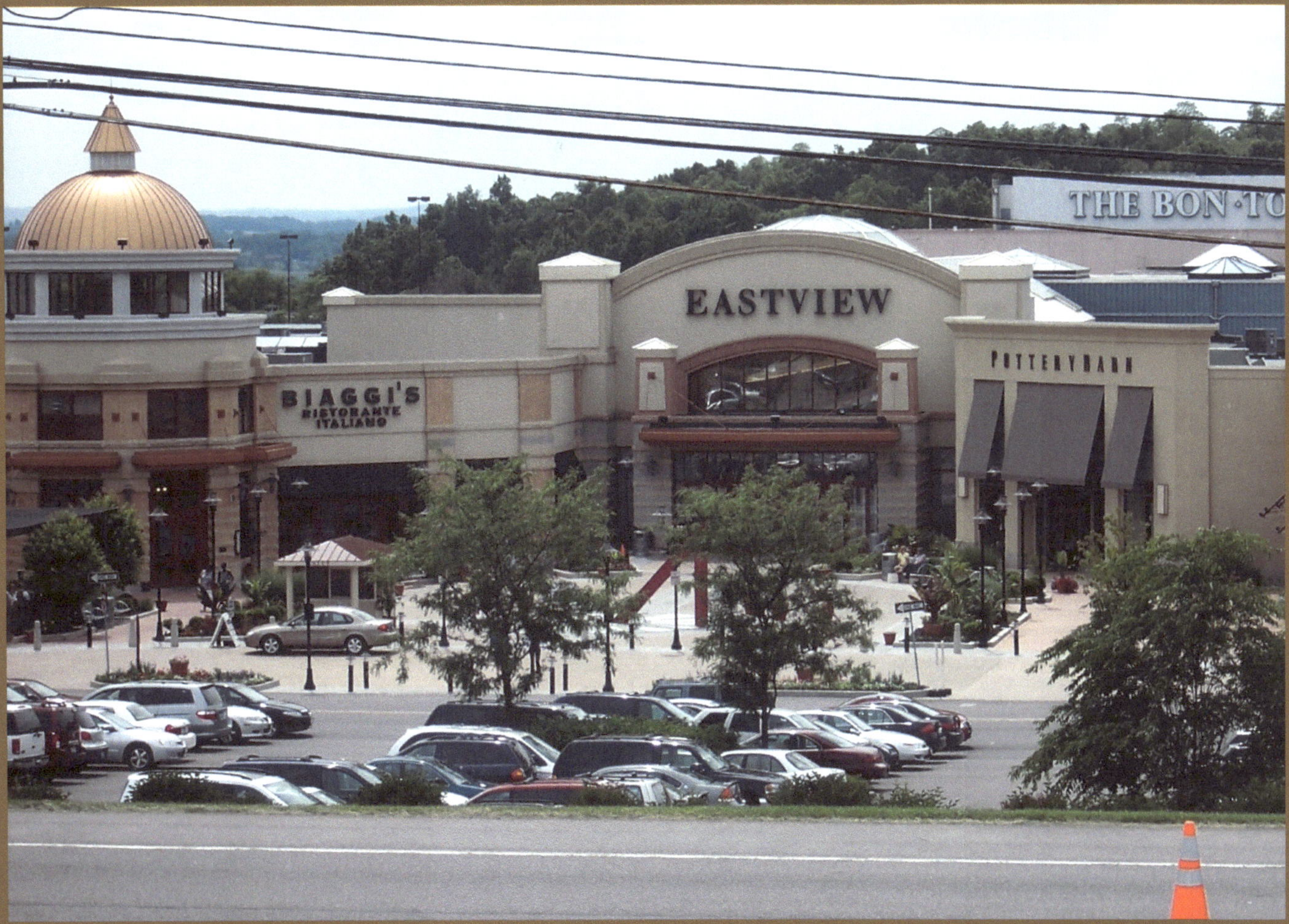

"Our passion is travel, and we want to share our adventures to inspire others to explore the world with their loved ones. Dare to live beyond the box."

Dates in the States

Introduction

Hey there! We're Crystal and Shane, the duo behind Dates in the States, where we share our love for discovering unique adventures, unforgettable moments, and hidden gems across the U.S. Whether you're searching for a fun date idea, a new place to explore, or just a little inspiration, we've got you covered!

Our Mystery Date Books are designed to help couples (and adventurous friends!) shake up their routine and experience the best local spots in a fun, intentional way. Inside, you'll find a curated collection of date ideas—each one meant to be completed over the course of a single day in a specific neighborhood. All of which are a surprise until you flip the page!

It's like a little challenge to break out of your comfort zone, support local, and make memories that stick. We hope this book helps you laugh more, explore more, and connect more—with each other and with your city. Let the mystery begin!

Here's What To Expect:

In this Mystery Date Book, we're taking you to Victor, NY—a charming Finger Lakes town filled with lots of shopping, craft brews and wines, and good food.

Here's what to expect for your day ahead:

Start your adventure with a cozy brunch at a charming local café, then take a stroll through history at one of the area's oldest landmarks. Next, head to Eastview Mall—not just for shopping, but for some unexpected fun. Wrap up your day with bold flavors and a festive atmosphere at a vibrant Mexican restaurant.

Whether you're exploring with your partner, your bestie, your kids, or even on your own—this date is all about making memories.

Start

Busy Bean Cafe

10 E Main St #106
Victor, NY 14564

Start your Victor adventure the right way—with caffeine and sweets. This cozy little café is the perfect spot to fuel up before the day unfolds. Whether you're craving a classic egg sandwich, avocado toast, or would rather split-a-muffin-and-stare-into-each-other's-souls, The Busy Bean has something to kick off this date just right.

Our favorites are their chai lattes and french toast muffins!

Once you're full and caffeinated—it's time to head to your first adventure. But don't get too comfy... this day's just getting started.

Second Stop

Ganondagan State Historic Site
7000 Co Rd 41
Victor, NY 14564

Time to walk off those breakfast carbs with a side of history. Just a short drive away, Ganondagan State Historic Site is a place that invites you to slow down and step into the past. This land was once a thriving 17th-century Seneca town, and today, you can wander its peaceful trails, explore the Seneca Bark Longhouse, and—if the museum is open—dive even deeper into the rich Haudenosaunee (Iroquois) heritage.

Find a spot on the trail or near the longhouse to sit, breathe, and just take it all in. If the museum is open, definitely head inside—it's full of immersive exhibits and stories that'll stick with you. If it's closed, no worries. Just being here is pretty magical.

Third Stop
Historic Valentown Museum
267 High St.
Victor, NY 14564

Tucked just behind the hustle of modern Victor is a time capsule waiting to be explored. The Valentown Museum isn't just a building— it's an entire 19th-century village under one roof.

Think: a general store, barber shop, music school, ballroom, and more... all frozen in time like someone just stepped out for lunch in 1890 and forgot to come back.

Heads up: This stop is seasonal and only open select days/hours. Be sure to look on their website for more information: historicvalentownmuseum.com

If it's closed, don't stress—you can still admire the old-school charm from outside, and maybe peek through the windows like curious time travelers.

Fourth Stop

Eastview Mall (with a twist)

7979 Pittsford Victor Rd.
Victor, NY 14564

This isn't your average mall date. Sure, Eastview Mall is packed with great shops, but your real mission here is to turn up the fun at DICK'S House of Sport.

Located right inside the mall, this place is way more than a sporting goods store—it's an experience. Challenge each other to a friendly race up the indoor rock climbing wall, take some swings in the high-tech batting cage, or see who's got the better short game in the golf simulators. Whether you're fueling your competitive side or just laughing your way through each activity, this stop is all about movement, connection, and making memories.

Ready, set, play!

Final Stop

Adelita's Mexican Cocina & Tequila

1002 Eastview Mall

Victor, NY 14564

Victor is packed with incredible places to eat, so trust us—it wasn't easy to pick just one. But if you're already at Eastview Mall, we say Adelita's Mexican Cocina is a must-try.

Start with one of their budget-friendly mojitos or a smoky Oaxaca cocktail (mezcal lovers, this one's for you). Then dig into flavorful enchiladas, burritos, tacos, or sizzling fajitas—perfect for refueling after an active day.

Still curious? Champps Sports Bar is another solid pick right at the mall if you're craving pub fare and a lively atmosphere. Or, if you're up for venturing off-site, head just a few minutes down the road to New York Beer Project for an awesome brewery experience with great food, craft beer, and cool vibes.

Alternative Final Stop

If bold Mexican flavors aren't calling your name this time, we've got you covered with a couple of other great ways to end your Victor adventure:

🍔 Champps Sports Bar
 Located right at Eastview Mall, Champps is a solid pick if you're craving classic pub fare, cold drinks, and a fun, energetic vibe. Burgers, wings, and plenty of big screens make it a great spot to kick back and refuel after a full day of exploring.

🍺 New York Beer Project
 Willing to venture just a few minutes down the road? Make your way to NYBP for an awesome brewery experience. This place nails the atmosphere—with craft beer brewed on-site, a full food menu, and a super cool setting perfect for unwinding. Whether you're into IPAs, stouts, or just some solid gastropub eats, this spot won't disappoint.

Add Your Photos

Keepsakes

Keepsakes

Thank you for joining us on this mystery date adventure! We hope you've enjoyed the delightful experiences and memorable moments we've crafted just for you in Victor, NY.

But the adventure doesn't stop here! Keep exploring exciting mystery dates in other cities and uncover new experiences across the U.S. by visiting our website, DatesInTheStates.com. There, you can purchase both physical copies and digital downloads of our mystery date books.

Plus, don't miss out on our Mystery Date Book Club, where you can receive a brand-new mystery date book every month!
Tag us in your date photos on social media! @datesinthestates

About the Creators

Crystal, the writer and creator, is a storyteller at heart. When she's not uncovering hidden gems for the next date night idea, she runs her own digital marketing company, helping small businesses improve their content marketing, increase visibility in their communities, and streamline their online presence.
Visit: crystalstatskey.com

Shane, her husband and partner in adventure, is a dedicated personal trainer and the owner of Beekstar Fitness in Irondequoit, NY. He specializes in working with clients who have limited mobility, helping them build muscle and focus on pain areas so they can regain strength and confidence in their daily lives.
Visit: beekstarfitness.com

Crystal and Shane have explored every U.S. state except Alaska (coming soon!) and are now visiting countries in alphabetical order. Whether road-tripping or curating Mystery Date experiences, they're always chasing their next adventure.

Local Love

A few local gems in Victor worth exploring on your next date.

THIRSTY TURTLE SPORTS BAR & GRILL
LOCAL DIVE BAR WITH OUTDOOR SEATING
7422 PITTSFORD VICTOR RD, VICTOR, NY 14564

BRISTOL'S GARDEN CENTER
FOR THE GARDENING & PLANT LOVERS
7454 NY-96, VICTOR, NY 14564

CHANGING CLOSETS
WE LOVE A GOOD THRIFT
7353 STATE ROUTE 96, VICTOR, NY 14564

Want to see your business here? See the next page for details on how to join!

Want to be featured?

MYSTERY DATE BOOK PACKAGES

—

Are you a small business looking to reach new customers? Feature your business in our next Mystery Date Book! Choose from our partnership packages below to connect with couples seeking unique experiences and exclusive deals.

Package One
LOCAL LOVE LISTING

A quick shoutout to show you're part of the neighborhood vibe.

Listed in the "Local Love" section of your designated neighborhood date book

Includes business name, address, and social link

Optional: Offer a small promo (e.g., 10% off for book holders)

1 social media shout-out when the book launches

$45

Package two
FEATURE STOP

You're not just a business— you're part of the experience.

Marked as a "Must-Stop" on a Mystery Date

Full-page feature in the book with your story, offerings and photo

Includes 1 social media feature — a dedicated post and story highlighting your business

Note: To ensure each feature is genuine and experience-based, we require a hosted visit prior to inclusion.

$95

Package three
PARTNER & SELLER

Be the spot and the source.

Everything in Tier 2

PLUS: Option to sell the Mystery Date Books at your location

Includes a bulk purchase of 10 books (yours to price + sell)

Keep 100% of the profits from in-store sales

Bonus: Tag as an official pickup location in our promotions

$150

Prices are subject to change

Feel free to reach us at any time by sending us an email to say hi and to learn more! We look forward to hearing from you.

| www.datesinthestates.com | datesinthestatesblog@gmail.com |

Sponsors & Affiliates

Our sponsors and affiliates help make our adventures possible! Explore the amazing brands and businesses that support our community.

Wanderful

Wanderful is a global community for women who love to travel. Connect, explore, and join a local hub near you!

Join our Book Club!

Join our Mystery Date Book Club and be part of a travel-inspired community, discovering unique local adventures together!

HomeExchange

HomeExchange lets you swap homes with travelers worldwide for authentic, affordable stays. Join today and travel differently!

Shop our books at a store near you!

Little Button Craft
658 South Ave.
Rochester, NY 14620

The Pawsitive Cat Cafe
120 East Ave. Ste 100
Rochester, NY 14604

Yesterday's Muse Books
32 West Main St.
Webster, NY 14580

Writers & Books
740 University Ave,
Rochester, NY 14607

Kittleberger Florist
263 North Avenue,
Webster, NY 14580

Flight Wine Bar
262 Exchange Blvd,
Rochester, NY 14608

Scents by Design
728 University Ave,
Rochester, NY 14607

Union Tavern
4565 Culver Rd,
Irondequoit, NY 14622

DATES IN THE STATES

A COUPLE TRAVELING THE UNITED
STATES ON A BUDGET

Contact Us

🌐

datesinthestates.com

datesinthestatesblog@gmail.com

📍

Based in Rochester, NY

CONNECT WITH US ON SOCIAL!
@DATESINTHESTATES

_____